THE
HEART
OF THE
MATTER

ALSO BY JOHN VALENTINE

Beginning Aesthetics:
An Introduction to the Philosophy of Art

Close to the Fallen

THE HEART OF THE MATTER

Selected Poems

JOHN VALENTINE

THE HEART OF THE MATTER

Copyright © 2024 by John Valentine

All rights reserved

An Imprint of Monte Ceceri Publishers

Cover photograph © Ed Eckstrand

Icon images from Vecteezy: "beauty vector lotus flowers design" by Evan Andri Suprianto; "swallow bird logo" by Joko Sutrisno; "hummingbird logo vector design" by Reza Alfarid

No part of this book may be reproduced, stored in a retrieval system, or transmitted by any means, electronic, mechanical, photocopying, recording, or otherwise, without written permission from the publisher or author, except in the case of brief quotations embodied in critical articles or reviews.

For additional information, press inquiries, bulk or educational purchases, and other resources, please contact Monte Ceceri Publishers.

Valentine, John, 1948– author
The heart of the matter / John Valentine
ISBN: 978-1-949512-13-7 (paperback)
ISBN: 978-1-949512-14-4 (eBook)
1. Poetry. 2. Philosophy, Modern, in literature.
3. Philosophy—Buddhist philosophy. 4. Philosophy, Modern—Existentialism. 5. Art and philosophy. I. Title

Monte Ceceri Publishers
P. O. Box 60623
Savannah, GA 31420
www.montececeri.com

Acknowledgments

The Adirondack Review:
"The Flying Wallendas" · "Michelangelo at the Sistine Chapel"

Amethyst Review: "Snow Geese"

Ash Canyon Review: "Excursion of the Deaf Class"

Dodging the Rain: "Love Song of the Hummingbirds"

The Fairfield Review: "The Great Santini"

Mudlark: An Electronic Journal of Poetry & Poetics:
"Ahab" · "Bean Field" · "Bouquet" · "The Dead Sea" · "Dervishes" · "Father" · "The Hands of Ché Guevara" · "Hands, Rise Up!" · "Heaven" · "Instructions for Translating Homer" · "Joan of Arc" · "Knots" · "Last Letter" · "The Pool Shooters at Burly Earl's" · "Praying Hands" · "Sobibor, 1945" · "The Sophists of Savannah" · "Suite for Jean-Michel Basquiat" · "To a Nun in Perfect Solitude" · "Tomatoes" · "Toulouse Lautrec" · "Trillium" · "What Rises"

Muscadine Lines: A Southern Journal: "Bee Father"

The Orchards Poetry Journal:
"Speaking in Tongues North Georgia" · "Winter"

Plum Tree Tavern: "Voices"

Pudding House Publications:
"Confederate Row, Laurel Grove Cemetery" · "The Last Word" · "Morning Glories" · "Straight to the Heart of the Matter" · "Wrens"

Red Eft Review: "Hourglass"

Red River Review: "Snake Handling at Mt. Zion Church"

Rock Salt Plum Review: "Flight 93"

Scarlet Leaf Review: "Walden Pond"

The Sewanee Review: "Bergen-Belsen"

Subtle Tea: "Chattooga River"

Zen Space: "Language"

It is only shallow people who do not judge by appearances. The true mystery of the world is the visible, not the invisible.

—Oscar Wilde

Contents

Acknowledgments vii

Straight to the Heart of the Matter 17
The Sweet Spot 18
Winter 19
The Flying Wallendas 20
The Great Santini 21
Tomatoes 22
Snake Handling at Mt. Zion Church 23
Speaking in Tongues, North Georgia 24
Instructions for Translating Homer 25
The Sophists of Savannah 26
Bergen-Belsen 27
Sobibor, 1945 30
Flight 93 31
What Rises 32
Snow Geese 33
Love Song of the Hummingbirds 34
Hindu Tree Marriage 35
Bee Father 36
Father 37
Michelangelo at the Sistine Chapel 39
Joan of Arc 41
Dervishes 42
Heaven 43

Praying Hands 44
Voices 45
Suite for Jean-Michel Basquiat 46
Hands, Rise Up! 50
Bean Field 51
Walden Pond 52
Excursion of the Deaf Class 53
Chattooga River 54
Ahab 55
The Dead Sea 56
Bouquet 57
Asphodels 58
Kingdom 59
Knots 63
Confederate Row, Laurel Grove Cemetery 64
The Hands of Ché Guevara 65
To a Nun in Perfect Solitude 66
The Pool Shooters at Burly Earl's 67
Last Letter 68
Toulouse-Lautrec 69
Wrens 70
Hourglass 71
Language 72
The Last Word 73

About the Poet 77

THE HEART
OF THE
MATTER

Straight to the Heart of the Matter

There's much to be said for the bluntness of bees. And certainly for the way a crisp clove of manure can snap your head back in the sun, like ammonia. Why settle for dissembling clouds, the rambling oratory of thunder? The lightning strike is what we want, everything clearer in that crystal moment of truth. The sudden illumination as stunning as Annie Oakley in her own circle of light shooting the heart out of playing cards, sideways, the target area less than a fiftieth of an inch in width, the round a .44 caliber fired from her Winchester Repeater, and Annie, dressed like the Queen of the West, quieting all doubt with shots that got straight to the heart of the matter. Her favorite clarification: a mirror, the sharpest angle, the Queen of Hearts.

The Sweet Spot

Remember how you used to catch
a fastball right in the sweet

spot? That pure, whip-crack sound
going home. Or maybe those

small birds swept in the eye of a
hurricane, riding sunshine and

stillness in the carnage. Right place,
right time. The absolute focal

point, like nirvana, a first kiss, even
that sudden right cross that

puts an end to the boxers'
discussion. Decisive, the

unexpected silence. And yours?
What will it finally be? Perhaps

an old friend in early spring as he
settles your ashes in azaleas

and phlox, the soft wind, the
sweet spot of the dead.

Winter

I would like to mention winter
without the coldness
of a lover turning away
or your dreams falling through
the ice.
Even way to the North
have you ever felt
the freezing as a friend
who can put you to sleep
and comfort you with a blanket
of snow?
Imagine a cabin far away
in the drift.
Imagine a wood pile stacked
high as a hope
while the wind whispers
it's here.
And all you can do is go back inside
and wrap yourself in promise,
like a seed or root
dwelling in silence,
waiting for the sun.

The Flying Wallendas

How delicately they eased the human pyramid
onto the high wire of danger, step by serious
step, the long poles seesawing, teetering this way
and that, calming then to find the middle way of
balance. All their faces rapt, lost in concentration,
the way a tiger slowly inches across a raging river
stone by slippery stone, his very life depending on
it. How they seemed a family floating in midair.
How Gravity was but an elegant ringmaster
tipping his hat in awe. They sailed across the void,
toed the very air. The crowd was hushed. Children
held their breath. How silent were the clowns.
And even Death, sitting in the box seats taking
down their names, had to admit that never in his
whole life had he ever seen anything like it.

The Great Santini

High in the wires of the circus, muscled
and mighty, he powders his hands,
pops his knuckles, and swings through
the air, hanging upside down like a
catcher of souls who suddenly and
mysteriously plucks you from empty
space as you're spinning and tumbling
and falling. He sends you sailing on a
thin trapeze stretched between death
and forever, wind rushing through your
hair, your eyes wild and free, as he puts
you down at last ever so gently, trembling
and shaking your head in amazement,
rapt as a child ready to climb the rope
and start all over again.

Tomatoes

I am prepared now to force
clarity upon you.

—Louise Glück

Is that you coming through the garden now,
the glories and the weeds,

in your old cotton dress, your ragged straw
hat? Have you come perhaps as

supplicant? Or benefactress? You misunderstand
our needs. The sun of course is

indifferent. We lick our red lips in vain, cracked
and dry. We wither. But your

old watering spout is beside the point. There's
a kind of love beyond

the light rain, the sprinkling. I speak for us all.
I am prepared to force

clarity upon you. Come nearer now. Whisper
in our ears. Hold us gently,

the way you have held new life, the small hands of
your child.

Snake Handling at Mt. Zion Church

The serpent rattles like dry seeds
in a gourd, coils in a dark box.

You've seen how grace stuns a man,
drops him with a quick hand, splays

him like lightning. The eyes of a healer
are feral, the yellow translucence

cold as a snake. You've heard the tangle
of tongues as they spit a broken

language wet with froth and sibilants.
You've heard the holy yammer.

But now the curling diamondback rises
in rings, spreads a necklace head

to head. It flicks a reed, fumbling for speech.
The pink mouth opens, finds

a sudden word. The spirit sweats, latticework
lightning branches in the

blood. Venom runs deep, rubs the bone, makes it shine.
They dance

the tarantella, their faces bright and blue as
a soul. They drop, go down

to darkness. What rises trembling then is pure,
newborn, as they shiver

and stumble, like Lazarus, to the upper world
of light.

Speaking in Tongues, North Georgia

Who knows the spirit's mutterings,
what they mean?
Bits of air, the froth and spit of faith.
You've come aphasic to the babbling
wind, the wild-eyed tongue,
every syllable of redemption.
Spuming verbs, hissing sibilants,
the midnight calling of the choir.
Cicadas know it, the buzzing sound
of the soul.
Or the doves' sudden whir
lifting in a shimmer of wings.
Cacophony, ancient grammar
of the gut. The rant, the voice
of all whirlwinds, vowel of all vowels,
every nerve of the ghost on fire.
The searing word, raw, primeval,
the burning bush of your heart.

Instructions for Translating Homer

Pyrotechnics, yes, the sharp cymbals of
swords, the flash of brilliant armor. Never

forget the gods, their charm, and treachery.
The sea is best. Sit down by the shore and

listen. In the restless waves the story of
mortals. Great ships attacking, wandering,

following currents home or to Hades. Courage
and betrayal. How the moon glistens on the loved

and lost alike. The rhythm of the words, fluidity,
dispassionate compassion. Nobility. Strength

of resolve in a time before evil. Follow the pace,
like dolphins in the wind. Racing, shining,

jumping now, rising to raise their heads,
as if to say, in sunlight or storm, everything eases,

everything's beautiful. Never rush. Lose yourself
and you will find him waiting for you in a world

of water, ebbing and flowing, nothing forgotten,
nothing overlooked, the great and the small, the

ocean coming in, going out, the endless story, the
timeless tides of our lives.

The Sophists of Savannah

—For Borges

Rhetoricians of singularity.
Disdaining dialectic, they have
come not for logic, Socratic
beauty, the essence of all
azaleas, but for each blazing
blossom, taken slowly, one by one.
Incommensurable, the unnamed
secret names multifoliate,
magical, whispered softly
only once by the wind, then
gone. The mourners, like passing
shades, tremble in the wake of
purely and precisely the most glorious
gods that will never come again.

Bergen-Belsen

1.

Gaunt shadows of wire
among the sheaves of skin
once called men,
loosely bound now,
tossed in the dust,
lacking a cord.
Swollen trainloads of flesh
bring the ganglia of limbs.
A loss of measure;
broken clocks run on time,
the execution of efficiency.
These are men who taste your fear,
connoisseurs of a sort,
sampling the pungent fare
of the grave.
Every gesture is clinical, disinterested.
You test the gauntlet, try the crack of rifles,
the fusillade of steel.
And like all martyrs who pale at the end,
who go down to dust
with the wild eyes of deer,
you talk of mercy with the hounds,
argue the logic of blood,
form vowels of pain now
for the deaf.

2.

Scattered days, the last pieces
of collage. Nothing familiar,
not days as we know them,
but strangers, drifting remnants
of clocks, the deformation of time.
Men face the machine like Robespierre
without glamour or dignity,
hangmen veiling their indifference
thinly, the endless sound of trains.
No romance in death,
mere work, the dull routines,
like shooting rats.
The end is thorough, disassembling
inexorably, tangled pieces left behind:
distant lives in lockets,
bits of hair,
the dolls from frantic hands.
The form collapses.
Flesh cannot resist the kiln, its dementia,
its dream of oneness,
like the cruelest sun
returning ragged men to snow.

3.

Let there be no sound
over bone and ash
in the weed corners
of the dead.
The wind is old here,
a low murmur,
the dry breathing through stones.
You hear the rasp, bending down
to catch the secret words of dust.
You touch the lives in cracking rock,
hands that gnarl in knotted roots.
The darkened eyes of lovers
are in the earth.
High in the currents,
swept by the ebbing sun,
a distant bird
climbs the last wires of light.
In the end, the utter still.

Sobibor, 1945

[L]ook at the soot on a white background.
—Daniela Danz

Snow, like a lie of purity. A shroud.
Nothing left. No scattered teeth. Or

glasses. No ragged shoes. Everything
erased by the moonlit machine. Soldiers

scrubbing memory, the walls. Shadows
of spirit. Bone crushers. The frantic

efficiency. While far away, up high,
beyond the smoke, the sky said:

*Enough. Some souls have to come back,
their ashes.* Look closer now.

A palimpsest. Traces of flesh. An old
blood painting. Handprint of a scream.

See the soot. The white background.
Before everything disappears.

Flight 93

—September 11, 2001

Sometimes love rushes
through the air,
racing like a madman,
crackling on the back
of electrons,
or riding a desperate wind
all the way back home.
The phone rings,
the last call
is like a whisper,
a hand caressing
your hand,
a kiss.
And all you can do
is listen
to the sudden night,
the silence,
the sound of sky
falling everywhere at once.

What Rises

What rises purer

than a snow-white egret,

wing beat filled with air

and light?

Gone now to wind,

pure ether,

blinding sun.

So like the bright magic

of death,

the quick scarf that rises

before our eyes,

the blur,

the sleight of hand

that sends a trembling dove

far away,

flying into thin air.

Snow Geese

What ineffable grace where they lift from satin
ice fields and arc across a milk-white moon

as if spirit had gathered the wind in this crystalline
moment for its own up-rushing, inestimable

purpose. What streaming they make along
the winter sky, how the air seems more mystical

and translucent for their flying as they rise to
greet the glowing sun and ride the canyon clouds

until they drift to nearly nothingness, a long
thin line of shadow and suggestion.

And then, as if spirit could never forget
the earth, they ease, hover, suddenly settle

into brilliance, glorious air, a chaos of wings
that feathers and preens the glistening light.

Love Song of the Hummingbirds

Impossible, you said. The clock races like a madman on fire

and death's like someone you lost a bet to and he wants his money, now.

Even sooner. Music in pistils and reeds? Blossoms? Not likely.

Just flitty ones with noses to the nectar. Only instinct. Obsession.

Maybe, I said. But listen: play the flutter of whir, slow it down. Put your ear

to the wings. What do you hear? Only Kali, the Dark One, goddess of skulls,

her ensemble of affection, emerald stick pins, batons keeping quick time

to the holy om, the endless raga, the marriage of beauty and death, the love song,

over and over again.

Hindu Tree Marriage

Garbed in the orange gesture of eternity,

the Brahmin has meditated

on all the raindrops of desire, the endless

gnats of regret. Perfection

seems to him to be a soft wind easing

through the leaves. Roots

deeply entangled, the arbors like arms

round saints and sinners

alike. Shading without judgment. These

are old souls, migrating

one last time, purgatorial, to their final

leaf-lovely bodies.

Words for the wind, a blessing, and suddenly,

in sunshine and shadow,

a glimpse of Shiva, the smile of Parvati, and

the Pipal and Neem

seem to sway, silently singing the song

of the world,

the endless wedding of all that there is.

BEE FATHER

Mesh-covered prelate

with a cloak of quivering

bees, soft hands sectioning

the hives into dripping combs

of honey.

Congregational buzz, whir

of nectar and wing.

Elemental host.

Even the queen hummed

in the hovering air.

The holy family spun resin

out of gold.

The father swung his censer.

Everything eased.

Perfumed that potted love.

Sweet, that shimmering dawn.

Father

—For Larry Levis

1.

The poem about your father. The one

about living in an infinite

house. The one about his name.

I know it.

Or rather

I'm standing just behind you, watching you move

toward death. A soul's length. What else

can I do? You and he gone.

Mine too.

I can barely move through the tangle of memory.

You're like a porchlight at the back of the house

of the lost.

You shimmer, glistening like glass.

Who could carve a better stone? This solemn

marker.

This life.

2.

Because you built houses

out of light

I'm at the door again.

Everything's open, windows wide.

A kind of pain pouring out,

love of the wound, beauty

running red in the blood.

You moved out long ago, moved on.

But it does me good to sit awhile

with you. I can feel

your shadow. How you loved

telling that the world trembles.

But now the door swings open.

Beyond the gate, the long road.

Shards of fire.

If I see you on the way

even air will burn.

Michelangelo at the Sistine Chapel

You must have been some
paint-splotched spider as you
swung from Adam to Jesus
high in the silk of your web.
Or maybe a yogi who laid
for endless hours on his back
making the radiant connection
between God and man. Was it
all there in the bright chapel of
your eyes? Let enough marble
fall, you said, and David steps
forth from rock. And here, in the
high heaven of your arms, was
it not the cut of empty space that
compassed hand and heart?
The heavenly host came forth
from trembling clouds. You were
high in the wires of your faith.

Were you not the parish priest?
The one who blessed the elements?
The one who came and stared,
who turned red and brown and white
to blood, hands, the very flesh of God?

Joan of Arc

> Give me the unfilled
> space between hunger and the morsel
> it can't quite reach.
>
> —Stephen Dunn

Because fire is relentless, we cannot
imagine its patience and délicatesse.

Its circumspection. Only that desperate
lust, the way it surges and strains.

How the wind is its enforcer, the bearer
of burning news. How the grass

crackles in its grave. But imagine something
cooler in the shadows. A secret kind

of wood as well. The kind that fire has
watched from afar, desperately in

love. Approaching slowly, because love
is cautious. Their vows are like tinder,

the purity of conviction, her gown hanging
its ashes in the air, the holy cloud

of smoke unfurled around her face. The lovers
entangled, rising in flame, the sear,

the sudden sacrament of desire.

Dervishes

If I were a Sufi for sure I would be
one of the spinning kind.

—Mary Oliver

Can a prayer be whirled to the sky?
Danced on the bright

petticoats of spirit? It's spring again
and the spinning

dandelions take to the air, leaving
everything

behind. Soaring, almost like
cirri,

they rise so fast. So high.
Could heaven

be a brighter blue? Lost in the blur,
can we ever,

ever see the Seraphim, their eyes ablaze,
lifting

diaphanous glitter on the wind?

Heaven

A cerulean sky that looks like it might
go on forever. No carbuncles either.
Nothing due or overdue. Just that pure
absorption with nothing you never had
time for. No Seraphim and choirs, no
halos. But really, what's better than
bright birdsong, the sun pouring down its
honey, the flowers a baptism in beauty.
What's better than an old projector endlessly
looping, playing that day, the one
you loved the most, over and over,
as if a clock had broken, as if tomorrow
would never matter again.

Praying Hands

They were waiting for Dürer,
beckoning, it seems,
for a careful caress to make
the ink glisten
on fingertips, the holy
reach out
from shadows. An Apostle's
hands. Meant
for another world. Penance
perhaps, or sheer adoration,
giving thanks for luminescence.
A steady hand was all they needed
to make their way from darkness
to light. To prayer.
To the silent sheen of faith.

Voices

> I an old man,
> A dull head among windy spaces.
> —T. S. Eliot

Sometimes quick clearings
in the night.

Palimpsest, traces trying
the language

of illumination. A time, a moment.
Then the sudden dark

of forgetting. You are like a blind man
tapping a cane

in his memories. Alas, the armature and its
shadow.

Stand up, quickly now, quickly. Here come
the voices, dry

whispers in the wind. Scarecrow, beware.
Where is the contract,

the guarantee of eternity?

Suite for Jean-Michel Basquiat

Better this immersion
than to live untouched.
—Lynda Hull

1. Heroin

So many derivatives. You knew

them well. The needle's rough

délicatesse, flowering ecstasies,

its promise always falling back to

earth. Never a new beginning.

Never. The gravity of it all. Some

kind of grace, though, in the ruins. If

I say tonight I love you, it's no more

pointless than the pain. No less.

Sometimes I think I sense you in shadow,

the breath of another world. Seized,

who knew the wages, the cost of things

better than you?

2. Notary

The needle was your imprimatur, flowering rush turned roseate, spreading like testimony to your face and beyond. Those were the dying days, each one a document, signed with the fiery ink of the spoon. Simulacrum. Only the ring of truth. So many ways to authenticate. So many. You made your own heaven. And hell. I always wait, look upward for the moon, that seal, the night's neon that burned through your veins.

3. Withdrawn

Thirty years later and I'm still getting
the lines. Your *Notebooks* kick around,
like you did. Come and go. *Withdrawn*,
it says. Release-stamped, sold to some
Florida gallery. Strange how words and
paint can flicker, shift. But never shimmering
spirit, incandescent. *Utsuroi*, you called
it. How everything's luminous, the most
beautiful, just before it's gone. Just at that
exact moment. Just then. I don't have to be
hooked to feel the pain, the empty rooms.
I don't have to be there to touch your
hand. But I am. Sitting on the floor with
your last hit, pain trailing away to some
other world. I think I'm a little in love
now. Maybe more. It's hard to hold a
shadow. Put my arms around the past.
You knew it: everything scatters, moves

away from everything else. Everything's
just a bit behind itself, falling behind, always
falling. Withdrawn, not even you could catch it.

Hands, Rise Up!

How strange it seems that so
long, old friends, you've risen

only for the ordinary, the usual
chores, your old grip wearing

the gloves of what must be done.
The needful, your dull duties.

How you've wandered, lost in the
pale thicket of the known. And I

as well, the bearer of no beautiful
songs. Two of a kind, you and I.

Weary. Until that stir, that gypsy
stir, those pure and pregnant

roses birthing everywhere all at once
their nurseries, rouged and redolent.

And how you'll stir as if from sleep.
How you'll lift, not toward pen or

poem, but speechless, toward touch,
like a loving mother, feeling your

way through light, caressing the silken
sheen, the trembling skin of the world.

Bean Field

[M]aking the earth say beans instead of grass.
—Thoreau

Cultivation by dawn and sunlit sweep. By hoe
and hand. Holy labor, acre by ancient acre.
Indian land once. Seeing neighbors now and
then from town. Advice: *manure in the rows.*
Puzzlement: *This is how you live?* All the gestures
received, graciously returned. And how the weeds
protested! How they objected to order. Geometry
of the yield. Clear the eye, see the truth. Plant
the pulses. In time, that crop, that risen crop, was
you.

Walden Pond

Why had no one ever invented a god of slowness?
—Peter Handke

A high hawk drifting in starlight, the
slow swing of clouds crossing

the water. Honeysuckle, the
perfume of peace, gathering

night air in the scent of stillness. No
oars now. His small boat

drifting in moonlit iridescence.
Everything speaking.

A threnody woven by tongues
in the dark. Croakers,

crickets, the late loon. Words
of the water. A slight

whisper of sweet wind, all
the risen voices

seeming to say: *Be patient, old friend.
We're here, we're here.*

Excursion of the Deaf Class

As if the wind were but a finger
brushed across their lips
and the rushing river only jewelry
with moonlight for a sheen
they rise among the shadows
in the silence of the stars.
A quiet candle, fireflies, the flicker
of the swifts gathering quickly
in the tops of trees,
luminescence on their wings.
The glowing world's like silver
in the air.
A pocketful of light, evanescent.
And everywhere the trace of spirit,
stirring now,
alive within the stillness,
sotto voce,
like the sound of rain
or stones
settling at the heart of deep
and silent water.

Chattooga River

—For James Dickey

Cold currents high up, manic, rush-
roaring from Carolina, boiling down

to Georgia, Lake Tugaloo. Churning
lather, water witches and roil. Places

only the daring go: *Jawbone, War-
woman, Dead Man's Pool.* Mount the

steed no one can ride. Angry froth,
bones shining in the sluice. Rubbed

clean. *Rock Jumble, Sock 'Em Dog.*
No prisoners. Cornered, the old stallion

races one more time, swings wild with
the wind. Headlong, bent for hell,

down it goes, like some great Appaloosa,
the last of its kind. Everywhere a halter,

long ropes, a saddle. Everywhere corrals.
See how the barn is closer. After so many

miles, see how the horse quivers, surrenders.
See how it stills, like water in a well.

Ahab

[A]nd round perdition's flames...
—Melville

Ivory-tipped and bound
by midnight mist,

by spirit-spout and moonlit
madness.

The sea roils. His heart of the
deep,

unfathomed. What lives
purer than

revenge? What cuts cleaner?
A reason

to burn. But hatred pays
a bounty

of the bone. Somewhere, lost
in the

maelstrom, he drifts, washed
by wind and rain,

by seething. The sea swells
at last,

taking everything away.

The Dead Sea

No prophylaxis for conscience,
none of your sins

sink here. Even the heaviest
things float,

everything bare, epidermal,
the sun like police.

The wide wave of deeds, memory
in the brine, burning

your face. Swim if you must,
dive, go under. No

matter. You cannot escape.
Salt is the truth,

rubbed on the past, pain of the
present. A little

tossed on the left for luck.
Or is it the right?

The answer is raw, the sear
of the kiln, the sting

of the sea.

Bouquet

Withering lives, like crinoline returning
to dust, falling, as we sometimes

suddenly stop on the keen edge of eternity
to follow a shooting star, or eye

the full face of an ancient moon, lingering,
if only for a moment, dreaming

of a different world, the way saints and martyrs
dream, the way we all will pause

with death in the wind, wondering if charred
roses, ashen and black, a lifetime's

bouquet, can be brought back to beauty, leaf-life,
heavenly hope, to glisten one last time

in the pure desert of the heart.

Asphodels

> I was cheered
>   when I came first to know
> that there were flowers also
>   in hell.
>
> —William Carlos Williams

Harsh, but not without compassion,
for they have known the days

in other lives where summer was for
bloom, winter for bone.

No more the délicatesse of violets,
silken lady's slippers,

Elysian phlox. They burn like ice
in the empty eyes of the fallen.

No memory of sweetness. Nothing
for lost and scattered souls.

Still flowers, but with bloom and blush
of smoke. Heart of fire. Damnation.

No growth, nothing risen. Nothing now
but char of burning beauty.

Kingdom

1. Morning Glories

An old man in his flower and vegetable bed, a saw
whirring in the latticework. Early echoes of the
hammer, plots of marigolds and tomatoes laid to
the sky. Hydrangeas and geraniums sending up
their signal flags, magenta and blue on green poles,
seducing the air. Morning glories, kingdom of the
seed and plant wisdom, ancient rituals, these
mnemonics of the earth. And now for this botanist
who slowly drops to dust, for this shepherd who
brings the small ones to himself, we see a blaze
of color where beauty opens, shows her love,
her small pink hands.

2. Roses

You will perhaps regard us only as an early blush of spring.

Or the gaiety of a boutonnière. Even a wristlet, assignation

of the heart. We are sometimes seen in the mouth of flamenco.

Or gently laid on a dear one who has passed. The black roses

of death. Remembrance in the dark. Masters of Ikebana know

us best. They cut our stalks and release us, fully free. Rootless,

we touch the heart of those who breathe us in. Perfume of

peace. Remember Buddha and his flower sermon. A blossom,

a smile, and sunlight shining everywhere, all through the House of Being.

3. Sunflowers

There, in the dappled dawn, I too want to rise in the sun,

swing in the sweet sway, feel the rhythm of deep roots.

Quiet calm, their faces full of light. I renounce all rights.

Claim no privilege. Let me lie down, live like beauty

in the weeds. Let me shine in the shadows. All night

I dream of silence and radiance. Moonlight alive on my skin.

4. Trillium

You are not the crown of creation. This you speak without
spite or malice. Only root tongue and leaf laughter. You shine
with your sway, the light encircling you like a lover. From out of darkness
you bring your bright star and glisten. Gently,
without effort. Come now, teach me more. How you rise on a ladder
to the sun. Words you whisper to the wind. Hold nothing back. The mystery.
Grace. That secret journey from seed to shine to dying light.

Knots

—For my father

Fifty years and strings still attached.
It's like looking through a window
at a boy getting lessons about knots.
That elegant method of showing
the best way to weave things together.
A father's infallible hands. Other lessons too.
Learning the ropes.

A death-knot and he's gone. So is the boy.
But older, the boy learned to tangle and untangle.
How to keep everything steady and work out
the hitches. His grip's in the hold of autumn
now, rust moving round the skin. His hands
shake, unraveled by wear. But ties still bind.
Old threads holding. The warp and weft of years.

Confederate Row, Laurel Grove Cemetery

—Savannah, GA

No angry hive of minié balls
tears at limbs now,
no sweat and steel
or red rivulets.
The bloodlust gone,
laid to rest long ago.
A scatter of dust,
the wind is low in the pines,
shadows linger in the ranks.
What can moonlight show you
of the dead?
A row of names, broken angels,
the endless rub of years.
Or stillness. That field of lilacs
and oaks dreamt of in the end,
its sweetness,
its perfume of peace.
Or summer roses
pinking on the graves.
Or widows once,
hand in hand,
remembering only glory
in the kingdom of weeds.

The Hands of Ché Guevara

are severed and pale under glass,
his enemies having made
a final statement
about classless societies.
A museum of symbols.
Garrotes,
pictures of gallows,
corpses swinging days from a gate.
But hands are a mystery
until an old story comes back—
How Booth lay dying by a barn,
spent like a cause.
How he asked the Federals
to raise his arms
and found an actor's hands
given whole to their fate.
His fingers were mangled and broken,
hanging limply in the wind.
How he shook his head—
"Useless, useless" was all he said.

To a Nun in Perfect Solitude

Reclusive, almost as if she knows
the glowing habit of desire is merely

memory, a path one cloudy day
long ago she could not take.

The dark raven she's become.
The silent shadow. She sometimes

dreams. Her dress, crackling blue
fire. Her eyes, ravenous. That

burning communion. That vault of
heaven. Those stars, just beyond the moon.

The Pool Shooters at Burly Earl's

Down to the nub. Grace of alcohol
gone to penance. Sweet consumptives.

Tangle of smoke in the air. No one
keeping score. Only Death taking

down names. The soon-to-be late
shooters. The early hours of eternity.

Closing time and they scatter and melt into
alleys, interstices, moons of the

neon night. Diaspora, like the whip-
crack snap of the last break, balls

clicking, flying, settling close to
nowhere, pockets still empty, the rack

broken now, the run almost over.
Everywhere, the chill of the night.

Last Letter

—Isao Matsuo, 701ˢᵗ Air Group, Kamikaze

Honorable parents:

Who but children could raise a toast to
death so calmly, silent as Samurai in

ceremonies of steel? Opening incarnadine
like roses on shimmering oil, all crystalline

and light, think of me in years to come not
as lost at war, but risen. Imagine the glorious

day, the scatter of flowers and glass on the
fiery skin of the sea. The wind skittering

like a whispering soul. Clouds will carry
my shadow and birds will remember

a brother. A eulogy of rain. But think of
today, the still of the sky. The silence.

And now, at this hour, the hour of departure,
remember: cherry blossoms glisten as they open

and fall.

Toulouse-Lautrec

I open a vial of gunfire.
—Lynn Emanuel

You were the poster boy
for machine-gun red and smoky
nights and the snub-nosed bark
of drop-dead blue eyes. The bright
blur of light was wild as tracer
rounds you lit like Roman candles.
Concierge of the carnival. Raconteur
of flash and pop, scattergun swirler
of pastels, the bang and bluster
of flesh-tone fury. Big guns then.
Kaleidoscopic blast of greens and
pinks and lacquered yellow. Explosions,
wild staccato clattering palette, ricochet
of sparks. Pistol-crack upon the walls,
now that smoke has cleared and all
the lights are out.

Wrens

Brown-coated visitors, humble enough
servants of the seeds we laid

in a trail to our door as autumn moved
through the trees like a rumor of rust.

First frost, everywhere the instinct of retraction.
Even the sun blanching in the chill.

Nothing brightening the plainclothes sky
or the garden settling in silence.

Nothing risen, though a sprig of birdsong
and the gatherers of alms were grace enough

to make you pause a while at the window
and smile.

Hourglass

Black widows surging on the shed door.
Newborn

but already deadly, the mother sending them
to warn

the world. So many coded messages:
the final fall

of azaleas, a rigid deer by the road, darkness
in a dying face.

Living life in the sun, you forget
the shadows. The years.

Inexorability of the clock. There,
in the grass, time

moving. The scatter, relentless.
The very hourglass

itself.

Language

Hold on to the center.
—Lao-tzu

Isn't it like running
headlong
into an early morning
spiderweb
and the more you
try to shake it loose,
the more it clings,
binds itself to your being?
Begin by doing nothing.
Does the wind rattle its bones
in desire?
Everything eases.
Take comfort in the spider who
weaves the silken strings
only as a means
to things themselves
and sits all day at its lyre
unencumbered
by the music of the wind.

The Last Word

Keening, who but the wind

will have it?

The vowels of its voice

high in the trees,

the sound of the sweep

of its verbs.

Its nouns naming your

shadows.

Tremulous echoes,

the parts of its speech.

The comma, the colon:

air like a period,

closing the door,

silently ending the sentence.

© Parker Stewart

John Valentine has a Ph.D. in philosophy from Vanderbilt University and taught at various colleges and universities for forty-six years, including the University of Alabama in Birmingham, East Georgia State College in Swainsboro, and the Savannah College of Art and Design (SCAD). He retired from SCAD in 2022.

He is the author of the book *Beginning Aesthetics: An Introduction to the Philosophy of Art* and numerous articles in philosophy journals.

His poetry has been published in the chapbook *Close to the Fallen* and in *The Sewanee Review*, *International Poetry Review*, *The Midwest Quarterly*, *Mudlark: An Electronic Journal of Poetry & Poetics*, *Southern Poetry Review*, *Snake Nation Review*, and others.

His poems attempt to capture moments of sudden illumination that reveal the interconnectivity of all beings. He has been influenced in this regard by Zen Buddhism and the literature of existentialism and also by William Blake's famous lines from "Auguries of Innocence":

> To see a World in a Grain of Sand
> And a Heaven in a Wild Flower
> Hold Infinity in the palm of your hand
> And Eternity in an hour...

Poetry is a dance between the universal and the singular, the one and the many. When we can suddenly intuit and grasp the dance, we come closer to empathy and appreciation for every life-form on our planet.

monte ceceri

In the early 1500s, it was from the heights of Monte Ceceri—otherwise known as "Swan Mountain"—in Fiesole, Italy, that inventor and artist Leonardo da Vinci let soar one of his experimental flying machines.

Envisioning a future where such fantastical creations would one day become reality, Leonardo desired to fill the world with awe-inspiring inventions and ideas.

Like its namesake's Renaissance roots, Monte Ceceri Publishers supports avant-garde writers whose works challenge current perspectives, inspire new paths, and speak to a modern-day humanism.

Based in Savannah, Georgia, Monte Ceceri is an independent publisher of books that raise issues of social, cultural, and philosophical interest, cross disciplinary boundaries, and facilitate cross-cultural dialogue through effective and engaging writing.

SwanHorse Press is an imprint of
Monte Ceceri Publishers, LLC

Printed in the USA
CPSIA information can be obtained
at www.ICGtesting.com
CBHW030739310824
13887CB00005B/213